SALT MARSH

WEBS OF LIFE

SALT MARSH

Paul Fleisher

BENCHMARK BOOKS

MARSHALL CAVENDISH
NEW YORK

The author would like to acknowledge the work of Paul Sieswerda of the New York Aquarium for his careful reading of the manuscript; Jean Krulis for her elegant design work; and Kate Nunn and Kathy Bonomi for their capable editing. He would also like to express deep appreciation for the loving, patient support that his wife, Debra Sims Fleisher, has provided for many years.

Benchmark Books
Marshall Cavendish Corporation
99 White Plains Road, Tarrytown, New York 10591-9001

Text copyright © 1999 by Paul Fleisher
Illustration copyright © 1999 by Marshall Cavendish Corporation

Illustration by Jean Cassels

Library of Congress Cataloging-in-Publication Data
Fleisher, Paul.
Salt marsh / Paul Fleisher ; [illustrations by Jean Cassels].
  p. cm. — (Webs of life)
Includes bibliographical references (p. 39) and index.
Summary: Describes the physical environment of a salt marsh and the plants and animals that live there.
ISBN 0-7614-0834-7 (lib. bdg.)
1. Salt marsh ecology—Juvenile literature. 2. Salt marshes—Juvenile literature. [1. Salt marsh ecology.
2. Ecology. 3. Salt marshes.] I. Cassels, Jean, ill. II. Title. III. Series: Fleisher, Paul. Webs of life.
QH541.5.S24F58   1999   577.69—dc21   97-26492   CIP   AC

Photo reasearch by Ellen Barrett Dudley

Cover Photo: The National Audubon Society Collection/Photo Researchers, Inc./Mark Burnett

The photographs in this book are used by permission and through the courtesy of: *The National Audubon Society Collection/Photo Researchers, Inc.*: M. H. Sharp, 2; Jeff Lepore, 6; Gilbert S. Grant, 9; Scott Camazine, 10(top); Gregory K. Scott, 17, 26-27; D. P. Wilson/Science Source, 22(inset, left); Leonard Lee Rue III, 31. *David W. Harp*: 8, 15, 16, 22, 29(top). *Susan M. Glascock*: 10(bottom), 12-13, 14, 18, 19, 20, 22(inset, right), 25, 26(left), 27, 28, 29(bottom), 30, 32. *Animals Animals*: Steven David Miller, 11(top); Harry Engels, 11(bottom); Fred Whitehead, 21, 24; Doug Wechsler, 34.

Printed in Hong Kong

6 5 4 3 2 1

It's a hot summer afternoon along the Eastern Shore of the Chesapeake Bay. Acres of grasslands stretch away from the water. These meadows are barely land at all. This is a salt marsh. Twice each day the tide comes in and floods the grass with salt water from the bay.

The humid air carries the tangy scent of the sea. A breeze ripples through the grass, making a gentle murmuring sound. A red-winged blackbird perched on a stalk of marsh grass sends out its loud, trilling call.

Most plants cannot live in salt water, so only a few plants grow here. Those few have adapted, or changed, to survive.

The most common plant in the marsh is saltmarsh cordgrass. Its scientific name is *Spartina alterniflora* (spar TY nuh all TUR nih FLOR uh). Cordgrass gets rid of salt through its leaves. Look closely at a blade of cordgrass. You can see salt crystals sparkling in the sun.

SPARTINA, OR CORDGRASS

Most plants can't live with their roots underwater either. Underwater roots don't get enough oxygen. But *Spartina* stems have hollow tubes that carry air from the leaves to the roots, so the roots won't drown and die.

CLOSE-UP OF CORDGRASS

BAYBERRY

TRUMPET VINE

Where the marsh meets dry land, the ground is less salty. Here we'll find more species, or kinds, of plants. The leaves of this bayberry bush smell delicious. Early settlers used the fragrant leaves as a seasoning and made candles from the plant's waxy berries.

Sea lavender and goldenrod color the border of the marsh with purple and yellow flowers. Trumpet vines and poison ivy climb the trunks of small pines.

MOTHER OSPREY AND HER CHICKS
MUSKRAT

A pair of ospreys has built a nest in an old, dead pine. One bird soars above the water. Then it swoops down and grabs a fish in its sharp talons. These ospreys will have to catch many fish to feed their hungry chicks.

This muskrat depends on marsh plants for most of its food, but it also eats clams, snails, and other small animals. Muskrats build sturdy homes using stems and leaves of marsh grass cemented together with mud.

11

Wind and waves form sandy barrier islands along much of the Atlantic coast. Vast salt marshes form in the calm waters between these low islands and the mainland. Marshes also develop along the banks of tidal rivers.

Marsh plants keep the water from becoming muddy by filtering the runoff from the land. Bits of soil and sand in the water settle in the shallow marsh. The grasses use the nutrients in the runoff to grow thick and tall. Gradually the marsh spreads outward.

The shape of the salt marsh is always changing. New areas of grass grow where the marsh traps more mud. Waves from heavy storms cut new channels. Old channels fill with sand carried by the storm waters. During storms the marsh absorbs the power of the wind and waves. This protects the land behind the marsh from damage.

GOLDENROD WITH MONARCH BUTTERFLY

People once thought of salt marshes as wastelands. Some marshes have been used as garbage dumps. Others have been filled in for building sites.

But we now know that the salt marsh is one of the richest environments on Earth. A marsh produces more plant food than the most fertile farmland! There are no hills or tall plants to shade the marsh, so the grasses receive lots of sunlight. Using energy from the sun, the plants of the marsh produce enough food to support a complex web of life.

A FLOCK OF ROYAL TERNS

Some marsh animals eat algae or the leaves or seeds of grasses. But the most important food the marsh produces is detritus (dih TRY tuss). Detritus is a mixture of decaying leaves and bacteria. When dead *Spartina* leaves fall off and land in the mud, they break up. Bacteria feed on the bits of leaves. Small fish, shrimp, mussels, and worms feed on the detritus. Predators, such as shorebirds, water snakes, striped bass, and blue crabs, feed on the smaller animals.

HERRING GULL CHICK

Marshes give animals a place to hunt, hide, or hatch their young. They act as a nursery, sheltering young fish, crabs, and other animals until they grow big enough to survive in deeper water.

RED-WINGED BLACKBIRD BABIES

PERIWINKLE SNAILS

Let's walk out into the marsh and see what animals we will find. Watch your step! The ground is wet and squishy.

Hundreds of periwinkles graze on the grass stems and leaves. The snails are not eating the grass itself, though. Using their rough tongues, they scrape off the algae that grow on the grass.

At the base of the *Spartina*, ribbed mussels poke up from the mud. The mussels keep tightly closed until the tide comes in and covers them. Then they open their shells and filter small particles of food from the water.

RIBBED MUSSELS

FIDDLER CRABS

When we step off the grassy part of the marsh, our feet sink deep into the sticky, black mud. The mud gives off a faint odor of rotten eggs. That's because it is rich with decaying plants and the bacteria that feed on them.

Look! Hundreds of fiddler crabs are scurrying across the mud. Each crab digs its own little burrow. All the male crabs have one very large claw. They wave their claws to defend their burrow or to attract a mate.

Thousands of worms and clams live just beneath the surface. When the tide comes in, quahogs and razor clams poke tubelike siphons out of the mud to draw in water. The clams feed on the tiny creatures they suck in. When the tide goes out, the clams pull in their siphons and wait for the water to return.

QUAHOGS

The tide is coming in. Hundreds of narrow channels carry the salty water of the bay into the marshland. Fish, crabs, and other creatures swim into these creeks with the tide.

The water looks green and cloudy. The color comes from billions of tiny one-celled algae called diatoms. The water in the channels is a living soup filled with plankton—tiny floating plants and animals. Plankton is food for the larger animals of the marsh.

Some plankton are full-grown adult animals. Others are larvae—young stages of animals such as clams, oysters, mussels, crabs, shrimp, and jellyfish. Most of the larvae will be eaten before they mature.

23

PLANKTON (LEFT); SHEEPSHEAD MINNOW (RIGHT)

This blue crab feeds on fish, clams, and worms. It is also a scavenger, eating animals that have died and sunk to the bottom of a channel. The crab's hard shell and powerful claws protect it from predators.

Blue crabs crawl along the muddy creek beds. They can also swim, using the flattened flippers on their back legs. Blue crabs hide in the marsh to molt, or shed their shells so they can grow.

BLUE CRAB

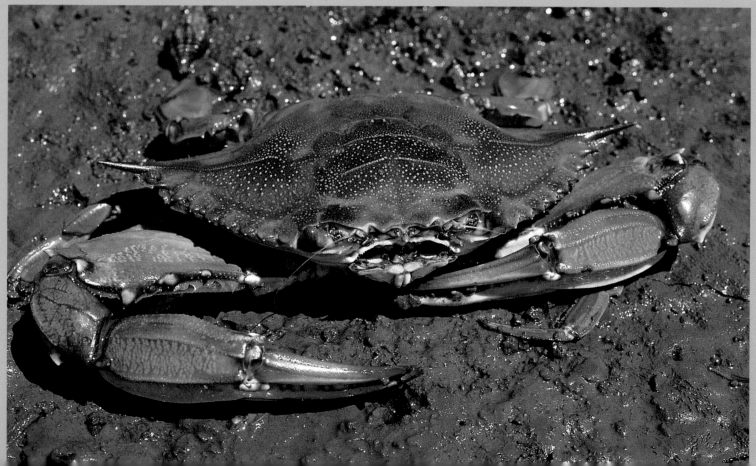

YOUNG KILLIFISH

The shallow creeks of the marsh swarm with small killifish, each about an inch (2.5 cm) long.

Killifish feast on the larvae of mosquitoes, biting flies, and other insects that breed in the marsh.

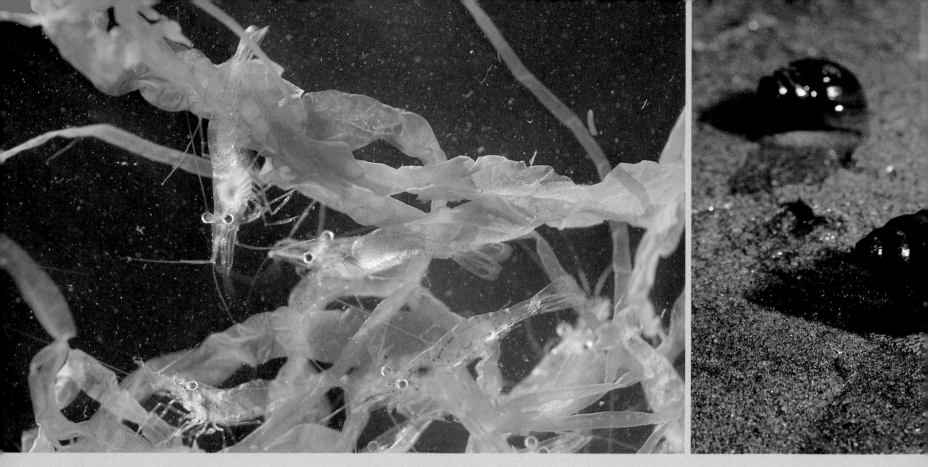

GRASS SHRIMP

SNAILS

Schools of small grass shrimp also swim through the marsh, feeding on plankton. You can see right through their shells.

In the shallow water, groups of mud snails crawl across the bottom, looking for algae to eat.

Stinging nettles, a kind of jellyfish, float in with the rising tide. They use their tentacles to sting

and catch their food. Be careful! The tentacles will sting you too, if they touch your skin.

SEA NETTLE

SNOWY EGRET

A snowy egret stands motion-less in the shallow water. It is waiting for a fish to catch in its long beak.

At high tide, large fish like this striped bass swim into the marsh looking for worms, crabs, or small fish to eat.

We may even see a diamond-back terrapin, a swimming turtle, stick its head above the water to take a breath as it hunts for snails.

STRIPED BASS

BABY DIAMONDBACK TERRAPIN

LOW TIDE ON THE MARSH

About six hours after the tide comes in, it goes out again. The falling tide uncovers the grass stems and the muddy edges of the creeks. We can see mudflats that were underwater only a few hours before.

WILLET

Large fish swim to deeper waters. Crabs bury themselves in the mud to stay cool, damp, and hidden. Shorebirds like this willet patrol the mudflats for small animals that the tide has left behind.

Each fall, the marsh is an important stop for geese, ducks, and other birds flying south for the winter. Many of them spend the winter right here in the marsh. They will find plenty of seeds, plants, and small animals to eat until the warmer weather returns.

The marsh grasses turn brown in the fall. Only the underground stems and roots stay alive. The old blades break off. The dead grass decays, adding to the detritus that will feed next year's marsh dwellers.

The marsh is cold and quiet now. Killifish, fiddler crabs, and other creatures burrow into the mud to protect themselves against the chill. Blue crabs leave for the deeper waters of the bay.

THE MARSH IN WINTER

In early spring, the marsh awakens. New green shoots of *Spartina* grass appear. The sun quickly warms the shallow water. Before long the creeks and mud-flats come alive with birds, fish, and crabs, here to feast on the bounty of the marsh once again.

SANDPIPER IN SPRING

Can you name the plants and animals in this salt marsh? Turn the page to check your answers.

Plants and Animals Found in This Salt Marsh

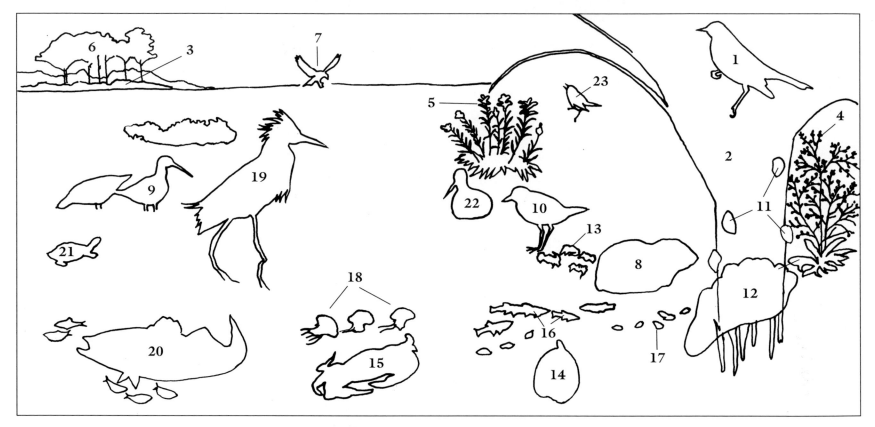

1. red-winged blackbird
2. cordgrass
3. bayberry
4. sea lavender
5. goldenrod
6. pine

7. osprey
8. muskrat
9. dowitcher
10. black-bellied plover
11. periwinkle snail
12. mussel

13. fiddler crab
14. quahog
15. blue crab
16. killifish
17. mud snail
18. stinging nettle

19. snowy egret
20. striped bass
21. diamondbacked terrapin
22. willet
23. seaside sparrow

FIND OUT MORE

Caitlin, Stephen. *Wonders of Swamps and Marshes*. Mahwah, NJ: Troll, 1990.

Ketchum, Mary O. *Clapper Rail: The Secret Bird of the Marsh*. New York: Henry Holt, 1996.

Pipes, Rose. *Wetlands*. Chatham, NJ: Raintree Steck-Vaughn, 1998.

Stone, Lynn M. *Marshes and Swamps*. Danbury, CT: Children's Press, 1983.

INDEX

ABOUT THE AUTHOR

In addition to writing children's books, Paul Fleisher teaches gifted middle school students in Richmond, Virginia. He spends many hours outdoors, gardening, fishing, or just exploring. One of Fleisher's favorite summertime activities is crabbing in the salt marshes of the Chesapeake Bay.

The author is also active in organizations that work for peace and social justice, including the Richmond Peace Education Center and the Virginia Forum.